The Divine Flow
of Abundance

HP

Hawkeye Publishers

Hawkeye Publishers

The Divine Flow of Abundance

©Copyright 2020 Jan L. Lynch.
All Rights Reserved

For more information, please address Hawkeye Publishers
HawkeyePublishers.com

Library of Congress Control Number: 2020920457

Paperback: 978-1946005472
Hardcover: 978-1946005496
Ebook: 978-1946005557

This book is lovingly dedicated to my spiritual leaders and mentors, Rev. Dr. Frank zumMallen and Rev. Dr. Terry zumMallen.

We met at the beginning of my New Thought spiritual journey, and they encouraged me to become a licensed Practitioner for the Awakening Ways Spiritual Community in Atascadero, California.

I am forever grateful for their support.

Contents

Introduction

Are you living with *just enough* rather than in Prosperity? How would your life be different if you were living in T*he Divine Flow of Abundance?*

Before being introduced to the teachings of *New Thought* and *Science of Mind,* my husband Patrick and I kept using the words *"just enough"* when paying our bills. We would say, "Whew, we have *just enough* to get by!" We did not yet understand the power of the words *"just enough,"* nor the mindset that accepted it month after month, year after year.

The two common themes in this book are *Spirit is your Source,* and *Be careful what you think because thoughts become things.* When Patrick and I decided to move north from San Pedro, California, to the Central Coast of California, which is less populated and incredibly beautiful, we were not yet aware of those two spiritual truths. People said, "You'll be glad you moved here, but it's difficult to make a good living in this community." Unfortunately, we unconsciously bought into that belief. Although we found jobs, we struggled financially for several years.

It wasn't until eight years later, when we began attending a small, independent, New Thought church in Templeton, California, that we realized how the words and beliefs of others affected us. We began taking classes on spirituality and reading uplifting, metaphysical books by authors new to us, such as Ernest Holmes, Deepak Chopra, Louise Hay, Wayne Dyer, and many others. We did our best to eliminate negative beliefs, and to limit detrimental self-talk. The change didn't happen overnight, but Spirit helped us create a very lucrative pet-sitting business for over 13 years, and I also blossomed in my career in the hospitality business.

Since life is a journey, not a destination, we continue to read and study to strengthen our trust in Spirit, and to deepen our understanding of the Law of Cause and Effect.

Our quality of life and the peace of our spirits improved so much that I was moved to share it with others. That's how I came to write *The Divine Flow of Abundance,* and it's why I am now sharing it with you – with love.

You are invited to join me on this potentially life-changing 30-day journey of learning to live in *The Divine Flow of Abundance.* It is intended to revive your unconscious memory of being created out of Eternal Love, and remind you that abundance is yours by Divine Right.

TOPICS COVERED HEREIN:

- Opening to the Divine to allow more prosperity to flow into your life.

- Using the power of the One Mind.

- Understanding how the Law of Attraction has been, and still is, creating your life experiences.

- Awareness that thoughts create things, and what you think is powerful, one way or another.

- Gratitude for the abundance you already have in your life will draw even more abundance.

- Celebrating all abundance, not just financial.

This powerful 30-day program offers the opportunity to refocus and realign your receptivity to Divine Order, use the Law of Cause and Effect on purpose, and to correct your unproductive self-talk so that your thinking does not sabotage your desires.

The Divine Flow of Abundance is a program that utilizes different spiritual approaches. Thus, each chapter includes the following:

- A metaphysical, uplifting message on abundance;

- An affirmation;

- A quotation of Spiritual Truth;

- An affirmative prayer.

By diligently immersing yourself in these daily affirmations, readings, inspirational quotes, and prayers, your abundance consciousness will evolve, as will your self-talk and, frankly, your life. Are you excited?

Let the journey begin!

Jan L. Lynch

NO MORE EXCUSES

(Read Morning and Evening)

Tempting as it may be to complain about not having enough money or ideas or opportunities, instead of focusing on what you think you lack, let's begin this 30-day journey by reviewing what you *do* have that enriches your life.

Much of what is beautiful in the world is absolutely free: your heart beats continuously, your lungs breathe effortlessly, your food digests automatically, and the world offers sunrises and sunsets bountifully. Allow these everyday miracles to help you tune into the feeling that it's entirely possible to create a peace-filled space within you that has nothing to do with money.

I considered writing *The Divine Flow of Abundance* for over three years before I had the courage to start. I had what I considered really good excuses for not writing it: I am not a writer; there are so many spiritual books already available; nobody would ever read what I write; and so on.

Eventually, I couldn't hide behind excuses anymore. Spirit nagged me to have confidence in myself, and when I realized the words would be coming from Source, I felt less pressured.

Once I felt confident enough to begin, I was guided. In other words, I first had to let go of the fear-based limitations that

I had placed on myself, and then I had to shift my focus and energy toward Divine empowerment and receptivity.

You can also do this by saying to yourself, "Everything I need to guide and direct me is already available within me right now." Reject self-limiting excuses that threaten to take you back to thoughts of lack and limitation.

You may believe you have absolutely no control over your thoughts, but that's not true. In *Excuses Begone!*, Wayne Dyer says, "Your thoughts are not located in your head. Thoughts are energy that is not found anywhere in the physical world."

The entire Universe, including you, is mental and spiritual. You are a field of energy, and your thoughts reflect back to you what you desire as well as what you do *not*. If you've been nursing self-limiting thoughts for years, it's time to implement a "No More Excuses" experiment by focusing your thoughts on appreciation, instead. That shift in focus and energy will draw *more* for you to appreciate so that abundance can flow through you.

Do you perhaps have a book within you to write? Or a screenplay? Or maybe you would like to learn how to play the trombone? There is only one thing you can do... begin!

No more excuses.

AFFIRMATION

(Repeat Twice Daily)

Today, I am aware of the abundance that surrounds me, and that the Universe freely provides with love. I give thanks as I express the bounty of Spirit all around me and in my life.

STATEMENT OF SPIRITUAL TRUTH

(Read Twice Daily)

"Everything has its origin in mind.
That which you seek outwardly,
you already possess.

— Genevieve Behrend

AFFIRMATIVE PRAYER

(Read Twice Daily)

I know there is One Mind, Infinite and Limitless. It is the Source and Supply of all things through Its immutable law. I am an individualized creation of Spirit, created out of Eternal Love to evolve and grow to my highest good.

Being one with this Mind, I choose to eliminate fear-based thoughts that no longer serve me. If thoughts of lack come into my mind, I shall refocus my attention on the limitless possibilities of trusting the Divine. I know the Law is fulfilling my life in surprising and wondrous ways. I am grateful.

I allow this to be so.

And, so it is!

IMAGINATION

(Read Morning and Evening)

You have been blessed with a very powerful and creative gift, a birthright from the Divine, and it's the gift of imagination. As Albert Einstein so eloquently stated, "Imagination is everything; it is the preview for life's coming attractions."

Imagination is magical because it can be anything from fun and whimsical to serious and contemplative. Imagination is creative in that it helps you visualize what cannot be seen, and anything can be brought into physical reality. It is powerful because your mind imagines the reality you desire to experience, which in turn, sets energy into motion for magnificent changes in your life.

Growing up in a small town in West Virginia, I would lay on the grass in the summer and gaze up at the blue sky and puffy clouds, imagining what it would be like to fly like a bird. Years later, I had the opportunity to work for an international airline for almost 20 years, flying all over the world. Was it my imagination that helped me get a job with a major airline? I believe so! My young yet imaginative mind was busy creating my future.

Sit back for a moment and consider what your imagination could create for you right now: a new career? A home with an ocean view? A loving relationship? Now, what is the best method to move your imagination into reality? In his book, *Wishes Fulfilled*, Wayne Dyer states, "Persistently act as if your dream is a present fact. 'Live from the end.'"

The same advice is included in *The Power of Awareness* by Neville Goddard, "You must imagine that you are already experiencing what you desire. Assume the *feeling* of your desire until you are possessed by it and this feeling crowds all other ideas out of your consciousness."

Your subconscious mind accepts as true what you *feel* is true. That's the importance of *feeling* what you imagine as if it's already fulfilled. This is not about thinking your desire into reality, but rather imagining and feeling the experience from the end result. If you can master that, you have what it takes to birth your desire. Go ahead and feel some more!

AFFIRMATION

(Repeat Twice Daily)

Today, I imagine my life filled with many blessings of friendship, love, and abundance. I feel myself experiencing each blessing with joy and gratitude.

STATEMENT OF SPIRITUAL TRUTH

(Read Twice Daily)

"Imagination is more important than knowledge.
For knowledge is limited, whereas imagination
embraces the entire world, stimulating
progress, giving birth to evolution."

— Albert Einstein

AFFIRMATIVE PRAYER

(Read Twice Daily)

I acknowledge Spirit as Infinite Possibility and Wholeness that is pouring forth joy, love, kindness, and perfection throughout the Universe. I am an individualized creation of Spirit, and I can never be disconnected from It because It is always present within me.

This Divine Intelligence working through me knows exactly what I need, and It supplies it when I need it. I receive my Good from this unfailing and perfect Creator. So, today, I let my imagination expand, allowing the Divine Presence within me to heal, prosper, and bless me in many ways. As my word goes into the Law of Mind, my imagination combines with the Law in amazing and creative ways. I give thanks for all the blessings and miracles I am experiencing right now.

I allow this to be so.

And, so it is!

WHAT IF MONEY
CAN HEAR YOU?

(Read Morning and Evening)

This unusual and important question is asked in the book, *Beautiful Money* by Leanne Jacobs. If everything is energy (our words, our thoughts, our beliefs), then it must be true that money is *also* energy.

In his pamphlet, *Money is God in Action*, Raymond Charles Barker points out that prosperity is the circulation of money (energy) in your world. And as Harry Emerson Fosdick says, "A dollar is a miraculous thing; it is your personal energy reduced to portable form, endowed with powers that you yourself do not possess."

How we approach the subject of money and prosperity in our thoughts and words is important because it's how we create our reality. If Leanne Jacobs' proposal that money can hear you is true, then money is energetically "aware" of what you are saying, which means a change in how you talk about it may be necessary.

Several years ago, my husband and I took a class based on the book *Spiritual Economics* by Eric Butterworth. At the end of the four-week course, we decided to start blessing money as it flows through our life. Now, when we write checks to the mortgage company or for utilities, we bless the envelopes before they are mailed. If a check arrives in the mail or we get money from an unexpected source, we bless it as well, regardless of the amount. If we find a penny on the ground, we pick it up and bless it. This constant blessing of abundance as it circulates through our life is one of the major transformations from having negative self-talk about our finances to becoming more aware of the previously-unacknowledged flow of abundance.

Review how you are sending thoughts about money energy to the Universe. Consider blessing your abundance and eliminating any negative statements such as, "It has always been hard for me to make money," or "I never have enough money," and so on.

Instead, remember that Money is God in Action, and say to yourself, "I have money to spare and share right now, and I always will, because Spirit is my Source, and the Universe is limitless." Say it with conviction; Believe it!

Your money is listening.

AFFIRMATION

(Repeat Twice Daily)

Today, I remember that money is God in Action, and I speak of money with love and respect. I bless money as it circulates in my life for my highest good.

STATEMENT OF SPIRITUAL TRUTH

(Read Twice Daily)

*"You can attract only that which you mentally become
and feel yourself to be in reality. You are either
attracting or repelling according to
your mental attitude."*

— Ernest Holmes

AFFIRMATIVE PRAYER

(Read Twice Daily)

I recognize Spirit as an infinite stream of ever-flowing abundance, perfection, and love. I am one with the stream that is creating my limitless good.

I bless the peace, perfect health, amazing wealth, and endless joy that is pouring forth into my experience. I have an abundant supply of all that I need, and I am willing to share my good with others today and always. I am thankful for the boundless blessings that enrich my life and the lives of everyone with whom I connect.

I allow this to be so.

And, so it is!

GRATITUDE

(Read Morning and Evening)

Meister Eckhart, a German theologian, philosopher, and mystic of old, once said, "If the only prayer you ever say in your entire life is 'Thank You,' it will be enough." This prayer, said from an open heart, is the doorway to a life filled with amazing gifts, such as love, joy, peace of mind, and, of course, prosperity. When you have an attitude of gratitude, all things are possible because your mind is focused on how amazing your life is at that moment.

There is a wonderful book by John Kralik titled *A Simple Act of Gratitude,* which I highly recommend. Kralik describes how his life was at a frightening low point after falling apart in many ways. When he received a note from his ex-girlfriend thanking him for a gift, he noticed how much better it made him feel. That gave him the idea to pull himself up by writing thank you notes, so he set a goal to write 365 notes in the coming year.

What happened as a result was amazing! Significant and surprising benefits began to come his way. There's even a section in the book about *how* to write thank you notes. Would you consider giving this a try? Either by mail or e-mail? It's just one a day.

After reading John's book, I decided to also send a thank you card every day. I felt so good about making time to express my appreciation to various people in my life, and I loved the response I received from several recipients. Many thanked me, but they also asked why I was thanking them. I still make time to personally write notes for birthdays, anniversaries, sympathy for the loss of loved ones, and my most favorite: for no specific reason at all!

When you are grateful, you have positive energy that emanates outward from your being. You become a magnet of sorts, attracting more experiences and opportunities that enrich your life, giving you even *more* reasons to be grateful. Challenges or problems are reduced or eliminated because, aside from applying practical solutions, you do not give them any power or energy.

Life begins to reflect your good back to you in amazing ways. There is always something to be grateful for, so go ahead... write those thank you notes!

"God gave you a gift of 86,400 seconds today. Have you used one of them to say, 'Thank you?'" — William A. Ward

AFFIRMATION

(Repeat Twice Daily)

I am so grateful for all the blessings in my life. As I give thanks from an open heart, I know I am in harmony with the Divine, and more blessings will appear each day. I shall say, "Yes, thank you, and more please!"

STATEMENT OF SPIRITUAL TRUTH

(Read Twice Daily)

"Gratitude is the healthiest of all human emotions. The more you express gratitude for what you have, the more likely you will have even more to express gratitude for."

— Zig Ziglar

AFFIRMATIVE PRAYER

(Read Twice Daily)

I acknowledge that Spirit fills all space and animates every form. Therefore, Spirit is the Energy, the Consciousness, the Absolute in everything. It knows only perfection, goodness, abundance, and beauty in all Its creation.

I know that I am one with this Consciousness. I am an individualized creation of Spirit. Today, I praise the abundance in all things, regardless of appearances. My thoughts, my words, and my actions create only positive results. I expect more good and therefore experience more good. I am grateful for the Presence within me that creates my good in the most amazing demonstrations.

I give thanks for all that I have and for all that I am. Today, I also give thanks for knowing that every desire of my heart can be fulfilled because of my trust and confidence in the Loving Nature of the Universe.

My life is amazing.

And, so it is!

THE UNIVERSE LOVES ORDER

(Read Morning and Evening)

Each and every day, we recognize organization in the Universe as It unfolds and develops in an orderly manner. The sun rises and sets, the man in the moon never fails to show his beautiful face, and we experience each season flowing from one to the next without any effort on our part. An orderly Universe is one of Spirit's magnificent gifts to us.

In her book, *One Day My Soul Just Opened Up,* Iyanla Vanzant says, "Order is the grace of God that brings us exactly what we need, exactly when we need it." (Even when we think we needed it much sooner!) The ebb and flow of your life becomes more manageable when you accept the fact that order is your Divine Right because it comes from the grace of God. That belief is more attainable for you when your mind becomes uncluttered with needless thoughts, such as fear, anger, remorse, or guilt.

Another important facet for peace and calm in your life is your physical environment. If your mind is unsettled, chances are your home, office, or vehicle are also cluttered. When you take a look around, do you see stuff everywhere and items in ill repair? How does that make you feel? Is your physical environment a reflection of your calm, peaceful mind, or is change in order? (Pun intended.)

In the summer of 2019, my husband and I read the book *It's Not Your Money* by Tosha Silva. Chapter Two includes a section called *Start to Clean Your House,* in which Silva says an important part of opening up to receive is *making room* for the new by clearing space for it. Although our home was far from cluttered, we still decided to take the author's challenge and see what would happen if we devoted an hour each day to clearing our physical space.

The outcome was amazing. I created a journal to keep track of all the blessings that came pouring forth, big and small: we received several dinner invitations to very nice restaurants; we were gifted a brand new vacuum cleaner from our neighbor; we won $630 in a 50/50 drawing; a consultation with my eye doctor was surprisingly free; and we were gifted a delicious pumpkin pie for our Thanksgiving dinner. We had definitely cleaned out the old and made room for the new!

This could be the perfect time for you to take action and remove the worn out, the broken, and the useless things that take up precious space in your physical environment. Out it goes! When you do this, see how much lighter and more positive you feel. Be sure to have a journal handy to keep track of the surprises that come.

As for mental clutter, this is a good time to review your self-talk and remove the mental clutter of negativity (more on this subject will be discussed in later chapters). You will find that the order you bring to your physical environment, when combined with the peace and calm in your mental environment, is a powerful shortcut for feeling the grace of God. Spirit has a very special plan for you, and it is all in Divine Order.

AFFIRMATION

(Repeat Twice Daily)

As I create order in my home and in my thoughts, I am opening to the grace of the Divine to fill me with amazing gifts of love, joy, and abundance.

STATEMENT OF SPIRITUAL TRUTH

(Read Twice Daily)

"The order of your physical environment is a reflection of the order or state of your mind."

— Iyanla Vanzant

AFFIRMATIVE PRAYER

(Read Twice Daily)

Today, I recognize and realize the grace of God is evident everywhere in this perfect and orderly Universe. I am an individualized creation of Spirit, and I claim Divine Order as my birthright.

Everywhere I look, I have created space that fills me with a sense of peace and balance. My mind accepts the truth of my being as I experience Divine Order in my daily words and actions. As I move with this feeling of oneness with my Creator, I accept and give thanks for all the ways this Divine Presence continues to bless my life.

I release and let go.

And, so it is!

YOU ARE MEANT TO THRIVE

(Read Morning and Evening)

If the world doesn't change, you can change the way you live in the world.

The universe is vast with energy that is constantly creating new probabilities, where the only boundaries are those created by our own false ideas about life. We often forget that we are dealing with a Consciousness that is Infinite, Eternal, and Unlimited.

The fact that you exist as a consciousness able to change your thinking and make new choices means the Infinite Universal Life wants you to experience all that life has to offer, from prosperity to success, perfect health, and loving relationships. It expects you to grow, evolve, and flourish in every aspect of life. In short, the Universe created you to thrive; it is your birthright.

To thrive means to prosper or flourish, not just financially, but in how you approach every moment. My friend Stacy is all about enjoying life to the fullest. Some of her adventures include zip-lining in Costa Rica, parasailing on Maui, and kayaking down Idaho's Salmon River. She loves this quote from the movie, *Eat, Pray, Love,* "You have to participate relentlessly in the manifestation of your own blessings." And participating is something Stacy does very well!

Thriving does not necessarily mean adventures like Stacy's. Life can be fully experienced in peaceful and quiet moments as well. Here are some ideas to consider:

- Each day, praise and appreciate the world around you. Show genuine and enthusiastic gratitude to the people in your life. Just the simple act of appreciation will lift your spirits.

- Dust off your dreams and believe in yourself. What is on your bucket list? The nudge you feel within you is Spirit saying, "C'mon, let's do this!"

- Take a break from e-mails, text messages, and phone calls for some personal time. This is a good way to re-energize yourself and focus on the dreams you want to manifest.

- If you find yourself merely surviving, you are not living the life that the Divine has intended for you to live. You were created to thrive. You were meant to evolve and experience your full potential by knowing the God within you. The Divine's desire is to have you experience a magnificent life.

That is Spirit's plan for each of us. And you must admit, it is a darn fine plan!

AFFIRMATION

(Repeat Twice Daily)

I am naturally relaxing into a new and richer dimension of living. I am celebrating the blessings of each moment.

STATEMENT OF SPIRITUAL TRUTH

(Read Twice Daily)

"Your perception of the world is a reflection of your state of consciousness. You are not separate from it, and there is no objective world 'out there.' Your consciousness creates the world that you inhabit."

— Eckhart Tolle

AFFIRMATIVE PRAYER

(Read Twice Daily)

There is an infinite stream of Good in the world and it is called the Divine. It is Eternal and Unlimited. I am increasingly aware of this One Presence, this One Life, and that I am created out of It.

I accept that the Divine's Intention is for me to thrive and live an abundant life. Today, I am consciously aligning myself with the outpouring of Spirit. I am increasing my expectancy of greater joy, happiness, and deeper peace. I have a more complete sense of the Divine Power within me, guiding and directing me. I give thanks for this new understanding of how the Presence of Spirit within me establishes my life in a limitless flowing of abundance. I am thriving and I am grateful.

I let it be so.

And, so it is.

AFFIRMATIONS

(Read Morning and Evening)

Here is a remarkable truth: every thought you think is an affirmation, whether positive or negative. Positive thoughts result in self-talk aligned with the life path you desire, and negative self-talk keeps you trapped in the circumstances you don't like or desire in your life.

The subconscious mind does not differentiate between an affirmative statement and actual life. Affirmations are powerful tools that program your mind to accept thoughts as reality. They condition your mind, your spirit, and your emotions, to feel the pleasure of your new story *before* it unfolds. And that, my friends, puts you in alignment with your aspirations.

The success stories of some well-known celebrities who shaped their lives with positive affirmations are posted on **thinkup.me** That website also offers many sample affirmations with the option to download a free app that records your affirmations in your own voice and even adds background music to them.

One of the celebrity stories featured on the website is of Jim Carrey, an award-winning actor and big believer in the power of having a positive mindset. Long before he was a successful superstar, he believed he would get there. Jim believes that nothing in this world happens without thought and intention behind it. He imagined his success and constantly believed in it until his **affirmations** made him the global celebrity he is today.

Another featured celebrity is Oprah Winfrey, who said that without affirmations, she would not have accomplished any of her successes.

A few years ago, my friend wrote a rhyming affirmation that she chants multiple times a day:

> *I am fit, I am healthy,*
> *I am Love, I am wealthy;*
> *I am healing, I am feeling,*
> *I am wheeling, I am dealing!*

We are vibrational beings. What we put into the invisible energy field called Life is reflected back to us. Changing any thought or behavior pattern takes at least 21 consecutive days. Many people stop before the desired results have manifested. When creating your own statements of truth, here are some helpful guidelines:

- Always make your statements positive.

- Use the present tense. Begin with "I am" or "I have." If you say "I want" or "I will have," then your obedient servant, your subconscious mind, will keep your statement in the future, just out of reach of manifestation.

- Keep it brief and specific.

Once you have written the affirmation, read it back. Does it spark a strong belief and emotion in you? Can you actually *feel* the joy of the outcome?

Make a commitment to repeat the affirmation for at least 21 consecutive days, twice a day, or more.

Consider propping the affirmation on your nightstand, so you will see it every day when you wake up and go to bed.

It's not enough to try to be *less* negative; affirmations replace negative thoughts and feelings with higher vibrations of joy, love, and appreciation. Positive vibrations from your reconditioned mind work like magic, attracting the people, resources, and opportunities that you need to help you manifest your goals.

AFFIRMATION

(Repeat Twice Daily)

I am using my mind as a magnet for perfect health, amazing abundance, and loving relationships. I am grateful that I am blessed today in many magnificent ways.

STATEMENT OF SPIRITUAL TRUTH

(Read Twice Daily)

"We cannot make affirmations for 15 minutes a day and then spend the other 23 hours and 45 minutes denying the very thing we have affirmed, and still get the results we seek."

— Ernest Holmes

AFFIRMATIVE PRAYER

(Read Twice Daily)

Today, I acknowledge the Divine in everything: the ground on which I walk, the warmth of the sun, and the magnificence of nature around me. I am one with the Spirit within me, and I declare my life today is bright and filled with promise.

My recognition of Divine Presence within me neutralizes any false or limiting beliefs I have accepted in the past. I am affirming that my life is overflowing with harmony, prosperity, and peace of mind. Right now, in this moment, I truly understand how my union with the Divine is helping my life evolve in amazing and miraculous ways. I discard any thoughts that limit my acceptance of my highest good, and I give thanks for all the wondrous gifts I am receiving from this unlimited Universe.

I know this to be so.

And, so it is!

DUST OFF YOUR DREAMS

(Read Morning and Evening)

Visualizing amazing abundance and success goes hand in hand with spirituality. Daydreaming about changing certain aspects of your life is not a waste of time.

We all say, "Oh, I would just love to... (*fill in the blank*)." Our deep down desires don't let go of us no matter how hard we try to push them away. Have you given up on a dream because you couldn't see any possibility of it coming true? If so, here's a biblical quote for you to consider: "With God, all things are possible." (Matthew 19:26)

In her book, *The Dynamic Laws of Prosperity*, Catherine Ponder says, "You may not have succeeded because you felt that you had to succeed alone, which overwhelmed you and it was easier to settle for failure." The truth is you are never alone. The dream, the deep down desire that will not go away, is Spirit encouraging you.

When I was in high school, my friend Carrie wanted to be a Rockette (a dancer in the American precision dance company that's been performing at Radio City Music Hall in New York City since 1932). It was all she talked about, much to everyone's annoyance. Carrie took every dance class offered in our small community, and she became proficient in jazz, tap, and ballet (all prerequisites for becoming a Rockette).

But she was still a small-town girl taking small-town classes. What were the odds?

While the rest of us discussed which colleges we wanted to attend after high school, Carrie only talked about being a Rockette, and we all just rolled our eyes. When she turned 18, Carrie flew to the Big Apple, auditioned, and was accepted to be a New York Rockette!

A year later, I saw Carrie in the line of Rockettes on television, performing in the Thanksgiving Day Parade. I could only smile and say to myself, *You go, girl!*

Where there is a will, there is a way. Aligning the strength and depth of your dreams and desires with the energy of the Divine is how you find your way. God can open the door to your dreams.

Catherine Ponder says it best, "Businesses have been saved, fortunes built, discoveries made, inventions perfected, and the dead restored to life, long after the sentence of defeat had been passed by humanity. Thank God that His goodness does not stop at the limits of our human vision. Keep steady, keep your faith, and keep your courage; remember that God opens ways where, to human sense, there is no way! Grasp this truth and hold fast to it."

So, dust off your dreams, keep feeling and visualizing the outcome, and let Spirit find the way. You are not alone.

AFFIRMATION

(Repeat Twice Daily)

God is prospering me now in ways I could never imagine!

STATEMENT OF SPIRITUAL TRUTH

(Read Twice Daily)

*"You can start with nothing. And out of
nothing, out of no-way, a way will be made."*

— Michael Beckwith

AFFIRMATIVE PRAYER

(Read Twice Daily)

I recognize there is only One Power, One Mind, One Creator in the Universe. I am created out of this Loving Presence and I am always connected to it as my Source. All things are possible through me because It is a Power within me.

I open myself to the wisdom within, knowing there is One Intelligence in the Universe. I trust this Power and Intelligence, knowing that whatever I need to know is revealed to me, and that anything I need comes to me at the right time, place, and sequence.

Spirit is unlimited in ways to manifest my innermost dreams and desires. It opens the pathway for me in amazing ways. I give thanks that I am not alone in my desires. I can release them to let go and let God.

I allow this to be.

And, so it is!

Chapter 9

BE LIKE SPONGEBOB SQUAREPANTS!

(Read Morning and Night)

As we see in many beloved books and movies, such as *A Christmas Carol* and *It's a Wonderful Life,* having a fulfilling existence means more than just having money. Fulfillment also includes peace of mind, a loving family or relationship, loyal and fun friendships and, yes, financial freedom. It all begins with attitude and, surprisingly, S*pongeBob SquarePants* can be a fine example of having the right attitude. Here are a few of *SpongeBob's* beliefs:

- <u>You can do whatever you set your mind to</u>. His not-so-secret "secret" is not letting other people's doubts discourage him from what he wants to do (like flipping patties behind the fry cooker at the *Krusty Krab*).

- <u>Own your mistakes, no matter the consequences</u>. Mistakes happen, people aren't perfect, and that includes *SpongeBob*. Sometimes, your truth is the only value left that can give you a second chance at redemption.

- <u>Find something positive in whatever you do</u>. Even when faced with sour and grumpy characters, *SpongeBob* stays true to himself and lets his spirit shine.

Even though he's a ridiculous-looking children's cartoon, *SpongeBob* is a perfect example of how your attitude defines your life. You either accept the good with your arms wide open, grinning from ear to ear, or nothing goes right because your attitude needs an adjustment.

During her remarkable life, Helen Keller stood as a powerful example of how determination, hard work, and a positive attitude can allow an individual to triumph over adversity. Ms. Keller lost her sight and hearing at 19 months of age. In 1904, she graduated from Radcliffe College with honors, and she was the first deaf and blind person to earn a degree. She went on to become one of the 20th century's leading humanitarians and co-founder of the ACLU. Regardless of her physical challenges, Ms. Keller had the right attitude.

Mental acceptance is crucial. If you've been setting your sights too low, they need to be raised. Just as the warmth of the sun and the beauty of nature comes from the inexhaustible, all-providing Power of the Divine, so is your unlimited inner source of love, perfection, money, and healing.

All that you desire is ready for manifestation. Go for it!

AFFIRMATION

(Repeat Twice Daily)

I am bursting with the fullness of life, with wealth, and with the unlimited abundance that surrounds and moves me into complete oneness with Source.

STATEMENT OF SPIRITUAL TRUTH

(Read Twice Daily)

*"When we learn to trust the Universe, we become happy,
prosperous, and well. We must learn to come under
that Divine Government and accept the fact that
Nature's table is ever-filled. Never was
there a Cosmic famine."*

— Ernest Holmes

AFFIRMATIVE PRAYER

(Read Twice Daily)

I acknowledge the Divine as a living, breathing, vibrating Consciousness of Love and Beauty, filling all space and time. I know that Infinite Intelligence is a living presence within me and within all beings.

As I accept that all my good comes from the Source within me, it opens the door for my immediate blessings. I have faith that all that is mine by Divine Right comes to me in amazing and unexpected ways. These blessings fill my heart and my mind with gratitude and love.

As I release these words of Truth unto the Law of Mind, I know that a full and abundant life lies before and within me.

I accept this as already so.

And, so it is!

TELL A NEW STORY

(Read Morning and Evening)

Instead of dwelling on the negative aspects of your life, tap into the power that you have to create a positive new story of who you are in the Now. Do you believe in the Law of Attraction, also known as the Law of Cause & Effect? Have you considered how your thoughts either attract or repel your desires?

We are vibrational beings, and our feelings convey our vibrational impact. When you tell your "old story" of negative experiences and perspectives, you attract more of the same. The Universe does not judge negative or positive; it simply responds to emotional alignment.

When my friend Diane was interviewing for various jobs in the hotel industry, but no job offer was forthcoming, she became frustrated and discouraged. She constantly complained about how she was never going to find a job, and that nobody wanted to hire her. Worst of all, she started to carry that negative vibration into each interview. The Law of Attraction was successfully working for Diane, but not to her benefit.

The old stories you tell others (and yourself) about your life can probably be re-framed. When you authentically create a new story that shifts you into the Now as a survivor, as a student of life, or perhaps as a determined person who seeks creative solutions, you alter your vibration. If your new story is a positive one that you can tell with passion, you can attract amazing manifestations that you actually *desire*.

You can then visualize your future life based on your new positive story. You can enjoy the process of creating your life experiences for tomorrow and beyond.

The Law of Attraction does not negotiate. The Law states that "like attracts like." In other words, the Law of the Universe gives you what you are feeling, not what you are expecting. Once you understand how this works, start playing with it. A good and simple place to begin is with parking spaces; just think and feel *There is always a perfect space for me,* and if you don't get a parking space in front of your destination, look for the blessing that comes from the walk to where you're going. As you become successful with that, you will be able to better consciously track whether you are creating what you desire or what you do not desire.

This powerful, always dependable Law of Attraction, is responding to you *at the vibrational level of your alignment* in all areas of your life. Does that mean an elephant will suddenly appear in your living room if you think of one? No, because that was just a passing thought to which you did not give much feeling, *and* one you do not truly believe.

When you tell your new, exciting, expansive, creative story, it's important that you believe and feel it solidly, down to your bones, and the Law of Attraction will have no other course of action but to say, "Yes!" It will then bring to you the essence of the subject of your thought, with details that may surprise you.

Wouldn't that be fun?

AFFIRMATION

(Repeat Twice Daily)

Today, as I align my positive thoughts with the Law of Attraction, I am open to clarity, creativity, and abundance. I am open to receive my highest good.

STATEMENT OF SPIRITUAL TRUTH

(Read Twice Daily)

In order for things to change, you have to see them as you want them to be rather than continuing to observe them as they are. You have to tell a new story.

— Esther Hicks

AFFIRMATIVE PRAYER

(Read Twice Daily)

I acknowledge there is a Divine Being operating through the Law of Cause and Effect. This Law responds to my thoughts and, more importantly, to my feelings. Today, I am telling a new story about my life, feeling the excitement of what is to be. I know that I am in alignment to receive my innermost desires, thus allowing the Law to draw to me exactly the big picture of what I am visualizing and holding in my mind and emotions. I can change my mind and expectations at any time, and the Law of Attraction will change with me. I expect the best, and I am experiencing the best.

I allow it to be so.

And, so it is!

ACT 'AS IF'

(Read Morning and Evening)

The previous chapter speaks about "telling a new story" in order to increase the flow of abundance and other blessings in your life. Acting "as if" is a continuation of that theme. The following quote from Wayne Dyer summarizes it nicely: *"The more you see yourself as what you would like to become, and act as if what you desire is already there, the more you will activate those dormant forces that will collaborate to transform your dream into your reality."*

This is not "wishful thinking," but a way to change your consciousness so that it moves in a more positive direction, thus changing your vibrational alignment away from the level of problem/lack and toward solution/abundance. All that you desire already exists in the Cosmic-Mind of the Universe. By acting as if your desires have already been fulfilled, you open the door of your consciousness to allow the energy of abundance that is *already within you* to flow and put you in alignment with all the good things that are waiting for you.

Years ago, I read a true story about a lovely lady in her 80's who had always wanted to take an ocean cruise. When she learned the local travel-agent was putting one together, she was determined to take the cruise even though she couldn't afford it. She memorized the ship's itinerary and familiarized herself with all the exciting shore excursions. She kept in touch with the travel agent, who gently reminded her that without payment, she couldn't take the trip, but she remained determined.

A week before the cruise, the travel agent called her and said, "You are not going to believe this! I just received a non-refundable cancellation from a client who is unable to go on the cruise. I told her how much you want to go, so she is 'gifting' her ticket to you. You *are* going on the cruise!"

Delighted, she replied, "I have known all along that I was somehow going to go on this cruise. My bags are already packed by the front door."

Now, *that* is acting 'as if.'

Let's say you are single and feel ready for a love interest. Imagine it is all already done: that someone's path will cross yours very soon, and all you have to do is feel the joy of knowing that your special person is on their way. Now you are in alignment with receiving that relationship. Act 'as if,' and be prepared for magnificent changes to take place in your life!

One more thing: sometimes people *think* they are ready for what they desire without realizing that there is some underlying issue of resistance dimming their vibration. For example, simultaneously wanting to sell your house, but also *not* wanting to sell it for fear of losing good memories from there, reduces the chances of it selling. If you clear up that underlying fear, the house will sell! So track any hidden resistance you may harbor, and keep re-reading this book until you clear it up. Divine abundance patiently awaits.

AFFIRMATION

(Repeat Twice Daily)

Today, I choose to act as if the bounty of Spirit is circulating as Divine Action in every aspect of my life. I speak my word, and Spirit says *Yes* to my declarations of new consciousness.

STATEMENT OF SPIRITUAL TRUTH

(Read Twice Daily)

"When you want to do a big thing, get the mental pattern, make it perfect, know what it means, enlarge your thought, pass it to the creative power behind all things, and when the impression comes, follow it with assurance."

— Ernest Holmes

AFFIRMATIVE PRAYER

(Read Twice Daily)

I acknowledge that Spirit fills all time and space. It knows Itself to be the Source of Abundance, Love, and Perfection. Everything Spirit offers is available to me as I am created out of and am one with this Loving Energy. As an individualized creation of Consciousness, I claim the attributes of the Divine as my natural birthright. Today, I am receptive to living an overflowing life of good. I feel joyful and radiant. All that I desire already exists in the Universal Mind and is mine to claim. I am grateful for all I have and will receive.

I allow this to be so.

And, so it is!

GIVE = RECEIVE

(Read Morning and Night)

One day, during the Coronavirus 19 challenge, I was standing in line outside *Trader Joe's Market,* waiting for it to open. The owner of the cafe next door offered free cups of coffee to everyone in line. It was a chilly morning, so the gifted cup of hot coffee was much appreciated.

After grocery shopping, I went into the cafe to purchase coffee, and I mentioned to the owner and his wife that one of the things our spiritual community believes is that "as you give, so shall you receive." The owner's wife replied, "I agree and also believe you can't out-give God."

The gracious owners of the cafe did not let their business being negatively impacted by California's shelter-at-home quarantine limit their generosity.

In his book, *Don't Worry, Make Money,* Richard Carlson says, *"Giving is an energy that not only helps others, but creates even more for the person who is doing the giving. This is a natural law that is true regardless of whether the person who is giving even realizes what is occurring."*

Your money is a form of energy. In order for you to be a magnet for financial abundance, your money needs to circulate and flow into others' hands. If it is hoarded because of fear, then you create "clogged pipes" within your mind, and then money has no inlet to return to you. When you give, whether in the form of a tip to the valet or a check to your favorite charity, you open yourself up as a conduit for the law that states: *as you give, so shall you receive.*

You can also keep your positive energy flowing by donating your time or talent. Here are some suggestions:

- Volunteer at your local pet adoption facility to walk the dogs that are awaiting adoption.

- Send a card to a friend or relative for no reason at all - just because.

- Sign up to deliver meals or purchase groceries for homebound seniors.

- Offer your time and talent to serve on a local non-profit Board of Directors.

- Become a Big Brother or Big Sister to a child in foster care.

Whether you are sharing your money or giving of yourself through acts of service, the Universe will repay you in kind. Remember, *"You can't out-give God,"* but imagine what the rewards would be if you try!

AFFIRMATION

(Repeat Twice Daily)

I know that everything I give with a grateful heart shall turn into blessings for me and others.

STATEMENT OF SPIRITUAL TRUTH

(Read Twice Daily)

"If we have given out but little and received only an equal amount, we can begin to give out more, and just as surely as we do this, more will return to us."

— Ernest Holmes

AFFIRMATIVE PRAYER

(Read Twice Daily)

There is one Presence, one creative Cause in the Universe, and It is Spirit, whose nature is to give through love, kindness, and beauty. All that I am is a reflection of Spirit, created out of Love in order to live a life that is filled with richness and generosity.

I understand that as I give, Spirit gives back to me tenfold. I open my heart to share my abundance of money, kindness, love, time, and energy. The good that I share today will be multiplied tomorrow. I give thanks for knowing that what lies before me is a rich, full, and abundant life.

I accept this as already so.

And, so it is!

THE POWER OF "I AM"

(Read Morning and Evening)

How many times a day do you utter the words, "I AM" without much thought? The words I AM, together with whatever follows them, create a statement that defines your life and your concept of self (from what you are to what you are not). Your life may overflow with statements such as, "I am not smart enough; I am a failure; I am not talented; I am not worthy; I am a mess..." and the list goes on.

Without realizing it, by attaching the words "I AM" to words that negatively describe you or your situation, you affirm a false truth that determines the world in which you live.

In her book, *I Am Source Code,* Janette Freeman refers to the concept of "I AM" as a powerful vibration we regularly use unconsciously, stamping "holy truths" all over what we don't really want to affirm.

In a recent conversation, my friend said to me, "I am not happy about going to visit my sister-in-law. I am not one of her favorite people, and I am always having to put up with her bragging about her children. I am sick and tired of hearing how well they are doing in school. I am not going to have a good time, and I know I will be totally miserable when I am stuck in their home for two days."

All I could think of was, *Wow! She is definitely not going to have a good time with that attitude!* But there was nothing I could say to change her mind or teach her about the power of "I AM" statements in that moment; she was too upset.

In his book, *Wishes Fulfilled*, Wayne Dyer said, *"The words 'I AM' are holy expressions for the name of God—the highest aspect of yourself."*

Since the words I AM declare what your life is now (and what it will be like tomorrow), this is your opportunity to break the habit of unwittingly tarnishing your holy name.

If the power of I AM is new to you, below is a suggestion on how to change your negative self-talk:

Give some serious thought to how you use I-am-statements in your daily conversations. Start by tracking any seemingly harmless yet negative statements such as, *"I am so sick of my job."* Try changing how you describe your current situation to, *"My job has served a purpose at one point, but it no longer offers me the chance to advance as I would like."* These words describe the situation without defining you as a "sick person."

Before you venture further into *The Divine Flow of Abundance,* commit to becoming more consciously aware of how you verbalize I-am-statements, and only use those two words positively, such as, *"I am open to unexpected blessings in my life. I am vibrant and healthy. I am a loved and loving person."*

And, so it is!

AFFIRMATION

(Repeat Twice Daily)

Today, I am noticing how my uplifting and positive thoughts help me grow and evolve in new and surprising ways.

STATEMENT OF SPIRITUAL TRUTH

(Read Twice Daily)

"By observing and teaching the I AM awareness, you will become more aligned with your highest self."

— Wayne Dyer

AFFIRMATIVE PRAYER

(Read Twice Daily)

Spirit is complete within Itself. It knows only joy, love, kindness, and perfection. It is Infinite Possibility and Infinite Wholeness. I am created from Spirit, and I accept that I can never be disconnected from It, because It is my Source.

The Divine Intelligence working through me always knows my greatest desire and what I need. I am using the vibrational power of my words to align myself with this Unlimited Energy and Consciousness. I receive my highest good daily from this unfailing and perfect Creator. I am grateful for all my blessings and for all the good that is yet to come.

I know it to be so.

And, so it is!

YESTERDAY IS OVER!

(Read Morning & Evening)

Although yesterday is officially over, much of the past may **not** be over for you if still carry past mistakes and disappointments in your mind. The past prevents you from moving toward new experiences. "Now," the present moment, is all you have. "Now" is where you put your energy in order to change, to move forward, to become the person you want to be. You are not the person you were yesterday. You can propel yourself forward by releasing the past.

In the 1993 movie Groundhog Day, Bill Murray is caught in a time loop, re-living the same day over and over again. He has no control over his situation, but you do!

Thomas Troward once said, *"Principle is not bound by Precedent; we should not limit our expectations of the future."* In other words, the future is not bound by your past.

Say it out loud: *My future is not bound by my past!* You are free to be a new you by releasing and no longer referring to *anything* concerning your past. We all make mistakes, but the past is done. You can now be loved, successful, and prosperous. Use your energy to focus on the present. You are alive, you have dreams, you have intentions, and there is a Power and Presence in the Universe saying "yes" to you right now!

AFFIRMATION

(Repeat Twice Daily)

Today is the first day of the rest of my life. I am using this precious time and my energy to focus on the present moment and all the blessings I am already experiencing in my life.

STATEMENT OF SPIRITUAL TRUTH

(Read Twice Daily)

"Life is for us today.
There will be no change for tomorrow unless we do the changing today. Today, we are setting in motion the power of tomorrow. Today is God's day, and we must extract from it what of life we are to live. Tomorrow, in the divine course of events, will care for itself."

— Ernest Holmes

AFFIRMATIVE PRAYER

(Read Twice Daily)

I recognize the Creator of all that exists in the Universe knows only the present moment. The past does not concern the Divine as it lovingly creates only in the now.

As I am an individualized creation of Spirit, I draw to me my highest good by opening myself up to the perfection of the present moment. Moving forward, I choose to see my life from a higher perspective, knowing that Right Action precedes every manifestation. I trust the guidance of my inner Higher Power as I step forward into tomorrow, I release my past, and I experience the constant stream of my highest good.

I am so grateful for my amazing life.

And, so it is!

Chapter 15

MONEY IS NOT YOUR ANSWER

(Read Morning and Evening)

If prosperity is a foreign or challenging concept to you sometimes, you may reasonably believe the solution would be to have more money. However, that is not the answer.

In his book, *Relax into Wealth*, Alan Cohen says, *"There is a theory (which is much more than a theory) that if all the money in the world was redistributed so that everyone had an equal portion, then within a short time, the money would be back in (or out of) its original hands in the same proportions."*

Why? Because money is all about consciousness; it's a mental game of how you see yourself in relation to abundance.

A long time ago, when ice cream sundaes cost much less, a little boy asked the waitress, *"How much is an ice cream soda?"* And the waitress replied, *"50 Cents."* The boy pulled money out of his pocket and carefully studied the coins in his hand. He asked, *"How much for a scoop of plain ice cream?"* The waitress replied impatiently, *"35 Cents."*

The little boy counted his coins again and said, *"I would like to have the plain ice cream, please."* The waitress brought it to him, put the bill on the counter, and walked away. The boy finished his ice cream, paid the cashier, and left.

When the waitress wiped down the counter after the boy left, she swallowed hard when she saw he left a 15-cent tip for her next to the empty ice cream bowl. The boy must have already developed healthy money-consciousness at an early age; he knew he had enough to share.

Having healthy money-consciousness means doing things that support staying joyful, calm, and optimistic, rather than living in fear or with guilt. A positive mantra could be: *Things always work out for me.* Otherwise, money will keep disappearing down the rabbit hole. The first step to abundance is raising your consciousness. Here are a few suggestions on how to begin:

- Regardless of what is going on in your life, there is *always* something for which you can be grateful, and now is an excellent time to acknowledge your blessings. Be grateful for friends, a beloved pet, or kind words from a stranger.

- Track the good things! Start a gratitude journal, a blessing box, or a bulletin board. Keeping a grateful heart opens the flow to magnificent and exciting ideas and opportunities.

- Replace the negative thoughts about your current situation with more positive statements such as, *I am excited to see how my life is improving.*

- Do the best you can to get into the *feeling* of having more than enough, even if it initially rings false. The Law of Attraction *never* fails. What you focus on grows, so let positive feelings be your guide to how amazing your life can be.

Watch your thoughts when you are handling money because money is God-in-Action. Bless money of any amount as it passes through your life because it is a movement of Divine Flow. To bless means "to confer prosperity or happiness upon." Your money is a symbol of abundance, not limitation.

Contemplate why you have had a limited belief about money up until now. Did your childhood household communicate fear around financial issues? Did you get mixed messages from your guardians about money matters?

Release outdated thoughts that still have power over you. When you put effort into tracking and uplifting your self-talk, your life begins to change.

That's how the Law of Attraction works!

AFFIRMATION

(Repeat Twice Daily)

I am developing my wealth mentality by being grateful for the blessings in my life and for the abundance that is flowing to me from the One Source - the Divine.

STATEMENT OF SPIRITUAL TRUTH

(Read Twice Daily)

"You can never create prosperity by talking or thinking about your lack of money. This wasteful thinking cannot bring you abundance."

— Louise Hay

AFFIRMATIVE PRAYER

(Read Twice Daily)

I acknowledge that the Divine fills all space. It animates every form, and It is therefore the Energy, the Consciousness, the Absolute in everything. It knows only perfection, goodness, abundance, and beauty in all of Its creation.

I am created out of this Divine Energy, and I believe that It intends for me to live and experience a life filled to the brim with all that is mine by Divine Right.

Today, I praise the abundance in all things, regardless of appearances. My thoughts, my words, and my actions, only create positive results. I am expecting more good, and I am grateful for the Presence within me Who creates my good through the most amazing demonstrations.

My heart is filled with gratitude and positive expectations.

And, so it is!

FREEDOM OR CAUTION?

(Read Morning and Evening)

What would you be doing right now if you felt totally free to live the life of your dreams?

Life is for us to enjoy. It really is! We have been given the freedom to make our own choices, to live a life of creativity, passion, and purpose. Ernest Holmes said, "Life is infinite energy coupled with limitless creative imagination."

My friend Shar was working for a mortgage company with a six-figure salary, living in a lovely home, and driving a cool Thunderbird – all the trappings of a successful life.

At work one day, Shar suddenly felt like a caged animal with an undeniably strong urge to get out and run away. The urge was so powerful that she took a week off work and spent it in the desert contemplating her life. The message she received was "Go!" Although a Higher Power within her was loud and clear, she needed a sign that the life-changing decision she was about to make was the right one.

The next day, she put her house on the market and it sold in less than 24 hours. That was the sign she needed. She quit her job, sold the Thunderbird, bought a motorhome, traveled to places far and wide, and never looked back. She says, *"Since the Universe and I co-create my life, I keep my mind open to the guidance that is always available to me. I may not have the answer to many challenges, but I know who does. For me, it is either trust or fear; I choose trust."*

Shar didn't choose the traditional path of living in order to experience prosperity. Freedom itself is Shar's abundance. She continues to travel to this day, trusting in Spirit, and knowing she is always divinely guided.

Stephanie Sorensen, author of *Unlimited Visibility*, says, *"Free yourself forever from the thought that God may be pleased by a life of sacrifice, that the world is any better for your misery, or that righteousness is more perfectly expressed through poverty than abundance."*

Spirit is not content with "just enough." Invite Spirit to direct your thoughts and actions to help you know your true value through meditation and self-reflection. You will inevitably experience new circumstances and situations. Let the Divine "light up your life." Spirit will create many amazing ideas and opportunities for you to enjoy in ways you could never imagine on your own.

Free yourself from old, self-limiting thoughts and actions. Expand your horizons to let many blessings come forth.

The Divine Urge for "more" is in you and waiting. Go for it!

AFFIRMATION

(Repeat Twice Daily)

I am always in a state of allowing and accepting. I am lifted to a higher experience of living.

SPIRITUAL QUOTE

(Read Twice Daily)

"One way to defeat limiting beliefs, even ones you may not know you have, is to simply dream of a life so grand that it couldn't possibly make sense. And then, start living that life today, however humbly at first."

— Mike Dooley

AFFIRMATIVE PRAYER

(Read Twice Daily)

I reaffirm that everywhere I look, Spirit is there reflecting back bountiful beauty, peace, and love. I feel within me a harmonious relationship with the Divine, and I know It intends for me to live an abundant life in many ways.

I accept the invitation from the Divine to live an expanded and adventurous life. As I continue to praise all the blessings in my life, the blessings grow and expand. My good comes in many forms and from experiences and situations I could never begin to imagine. I give thanks for all that I have, for all that I am, and for all that I am becoming.

I allow it to be so.

And, so it is!

DON'T WORRY – BE HAPPY!

(Read Morning and Evening)

Bobby McFerrin sang, *"In every life we have some trouble, but when you worry, you make it double."*

What are you worried about right now? Is it about an imaginary situation or condition that doesn't actually exist? Worries today create your experiences tomorrow, and who wants to keep recreating worrisome situations?

Albert Einstein said, *"No problem can be solved from the same level of consciousness that created it."* Thinking of ways to solve a problem that is within your control to solve does not qualify as worrying, but chewing on a thought with fear or anger, that's what worrying feels like.

Do you think that if you worry enough, the bad things will not happen or will go away? That is simply not how it works.

Set aside 30 minutes each day to worry. I actually keep my worrying confined to the same 30-minute time slot every day; it's on my calendar.

I've read a study that separated participants into two groups: one was told to schedule a limited time to worry, and the other group was told to continue worrying as usual. Those who scheduled their time to worry experienced a significant decrease in anxiety compared to the control group.

I have learned to laugh at myself when I found something to worry about during the day. I would stop and remind myself that "worry-time" is over until 8:00 am the following day.

It may not be easy to stop worrying, but it's important to try. Worrying causes stress and anxiety in your body, which can negatively affect your health. In the long run, worrying doesn't solve anything, it only creates more to worry about.

All we ever have is the present moment. Everything else is in the past or in the imagined future. If you catch yourself worrying, try saying to yourself, *"Things have a way of working out for me,"* and let it go. If you don't believe it, say, *"I can't wait to see how this works out!"*

Set aside 30 minutes a day for worrying, and then release whatever has been worrying you for the rest of the day. Breathe, smile, distract yourself, laugh out loud, choose to be happy. Be in the moment. The Higher Power within you has your back!

You have the ability to move above the worry. Give yourself a spiritual lift by remembering that whatever is in your mind will also be in your life.... very soon... It can be fabulous or disastrous, it all depends on you.

AFFIRMATION

(Repeat Twice Daily)

The Mind within me, being the Divine, knows only now, this present and perfect moment. I choose to live in this moment and to be grateful for the fullness of the life being expressed through me.

STATEMENT OF SPIRITUAL TRUTH

(Read Twice Daily)

"Nothing in the Universe denies your right to be happy."

— Ernest Holmes

AFFIRMATIVE PRAYER

(Read Twice Daily)

The Spirit of God is present everywhere, undivided, and indivisible. For God, the concepts of past or future don't exist, there is only the present moment.

As an individualized creation of the Divine, I rejoice in this present moment, knowing it is intended as a gift for me from the Divine. I accept that as I live my life affirmatively, I am happy. All the good that is filling my life is a completion of a circle, the fulfillment of my desires. I cast away all fear or worry that keeps me from my highest good. I am grateful for my life and how it is evolving.

I allow it to be so.

And, so it is!

REAL WORLD MIRACLES

(Read Morning and Evening)

Would you recognize a miracle if you saw one? According to the New Testament, *"with God, all things are possible,"* which leaves nothing out. Do you believe miracles happen in this day and age? If so, can *we create* miracles in our lives?

Have you ever considered that you've been creating miracles without claiming them as such? When something wonderful happens out of the blue, do you wonder where it came from? It came from you! Without realizing it, you have aligned your mind, your consciousness, your desire, with your Higher Power, manifesting the so-called "miracle."

In 1987, when my husband and I decided to move to California's Central Coast, I sent my resume to hotels in the area that were large enough to have a Sales Department. At the time, we only knew three people in the county. I had no idea how I was going to get an interview, let alone a job, because the odds were stacked against me. But our desire to move to this beautiful area was so strong, I just knew a job would somehow materialize. As Han Solo said in the original *Star Wars, "Don't tell me the odds; never tell me the odds!"*

Well, my sister-in-law gave my resume to a friend who was roommates with the Manager of an oceanfront hotel, and before long, I got the job. I thought, *Wow! A miracle!*

When you open yourself up to all the possibilities life has to offer, nothing is too big for Spirit, and nothing is impossible. If you can do that, then creating miracles becomes a common experience.

Everything is energy, especially your thoughts, which is why it is imperative to guard your thoughts by keeping them tuned into the life you expect and deserve.

In *The Spontaneous Fulfillment of Desire,* Deepak Chopra says, *"Beyond your physical self, beyond your thoughts and emotions, there lays a realm within you that is pure potential. From this place, anything and everything is possible. Even miracles. Especially miracles."*

AFFIRMATION

(Repeat Twice Daily)

I am aware that my expressions of love and kindness to myself and others create beautiful miracles in my life each day. I am open to the miraculous!

STATEMENT OF SPIRITUAL TRUTH

(Read Twice Daily)

"The secret behind miracles is that the person performing them begins without any knowledge of how they will succeed... yet they still begin."

— Mike Dooley

AFFIRMATIVE PRAYER

(Read Twice Daily)

I recognize Spirit as a river flowing through the Universe as Love, Divine Right Action, and Divine Intelligence. I accept that I am a miracle created out of the Divine, and I know I can never be disconnected from It.

The Divine Intelligence that is moving through me always knows exactly what I need, and my needs are always fulfilled through Spirit's miraculous and loving ways. This Divine Wholeness flows through me into ever-widening manifestations of love, harmony, peace of mind, and abundance. I am calm, knowing all is well with my soul, my spirit, and my mind. My life is truly miraculous!

I accept this to be so.

And, so it is!

THE POWER OF INTENTION

(Read Morning & Evening)

Setting an intention is different from setting a goal. Goals are usually rooted in a sense that something is missing or lacking in your life, and so you take specific steps to achieve a goal with determination to fill that void. The power of intention is not something you "do," it's a force that exists in the universe as a field of energy that creates the path of doing. Wayne Dyer believed intention is a force (energy) that we all have within us. *"Intention is a field of energy that flows invisibly beyond the reach of our normal, everyday habitual patterns."* If that is true, then manifestation depends on our ability to align ourselves, our consciousness, our personal energies, and our thoughts, with this field of powerful energy.

One way to do that is to act *"as if"* your desire for a happier, healthier, more prosperous life is already happening right now. Here's a rhyme to help you remember:

Think from the end;
feel yourself living the life you intend.

Intention is simultaneously creative and dependable. As long as you are in alignment with it, you can trust it to manifest what you seek into form.

Wayne Dyer also said, *"The way to establish a relationship with Spirit is to continuously contemplate yourself as being surrounded by the conditions you wish to produce."*

Several years ago, my friend Leila and her husband decided to purchase a new home. Although their realtor showed them many houses, Leila's vision of the home she desired was just not materializing. Being a very spiritual person and familiar with Wayne Dyer's belief that intention is an invisible form of energy, Leila decided to use this power to find the home of her dreams.

One day, Leila saw a house with which she immediately fell in love; it was the exact architectural design she had envisioned, but it wasn't for sale!

During the following few months, Leila drove by that house every day, visualizing herself and her husband living on the property, until one day, there was a "For Sale" sign on the front lawn.

By "thinking from the end" and setting an intention, Leila trusted Spirit to provide the path for her manifestation.

Now is a perfect time for you to "think from the end;" contemplate the conditions that you wish to intend.

Expect amazing results!

AFFIRMATION

(Repeat Twice Daily)

I see myself surrounded by all the conditions I intend to produce for perfect health and increased abundance.

STATEMENT OF SPIRITUAL TRUTH

(Read Twice Daily)

"Intention is something that I believe we can feel, connect with, know, and trust. It is an inner awareness that we explicitly feel, and yet at the same time, cannot truly describe with words."

— Wayne Dyer

AFFIRMATIVE PRAYER

(Read Twice Daily)

There is only Spirit, complete within Itself. It knows only joy, love, kindness, and perfection. It is Infinite Possibility and Infinite Wholeness.

Created from Spirit, I am never disconnected from It, because It is my Source. I believe in the power of intention as an invisible field of energy within me and the Universe. I am willing to align my thoughts and inner feelings to be in harmony with it. I trust the power of intention to provide the form, timing, and conditions for amazing manifestations. All things are possible through me because the intention within me is doing the work. I give thanks for my relationship with this power.

I allow it to be so.

And, so it is!

HOW ABUNDANT CAN YOU FEEL?

(Read Morning and Evening)

Does your checking account have to be overflowing in order for you to feel and express abundance? To consider yourself a "rich" person, do you need to be driving a flashy car or live in an impressive home? If your answer is *Yes* to those questions, then perhaps you can contemplate how abundant you already are *right now* in so many other ways, even if you're not a millionaire. By expanding your awareness of the unlimited Universe, more prosperity will be available and possible for you.

Abundance-consciousness means being aware of the existence of abundance already around you right now, and being able to connect to it. You are part of an expansive, ever-evolving Universe, whose desire is for you to be grateful for where you are while knowing that much more is available: new opportunities, visions, ideas, and more abundance.

My friend Tom is a successful attorney, married to a lovely lady with whom he has three terrific kids, and they live in a large, beautiful home in an affluent neighborhood. I asked him when in his life he felt abundant, and his answer surprised me. He said that having more money means having more bills, more responsibilities, more future planning for the children, and so on. When he and his wife first got married and lived in a small house, paid for everything with cash, and were excited about the future, even though they were not yet "wealthy," he remembers *feeling* abundant.

Abundance is a *feeling* about life and being grateful for what we have and where we are in the moment.

Imagine how different your life can be right now if you open to unlimited possibilities. Imagine how financial freedom will feel when you consciously choose to uplift your level of expectation with a few changes in your thoughts and words.

- Remind yourself daily that abundance is your true nature and rightful inheritance.

- Accept that you were born to experience all the blessings of the Universe.

Set your desires with gratitude. Allow yourself to be the channel through which the Universe creates your good. The details will be revealed later... and they may surprise you!

Thoughts become things, so be careful what you think. Keep yourself open to your good through a consciousness of gratitude, love, and trust. And, finally, remember you are not trying to *make* anything happen. You are simply releasing the abundance that is already within you, has always been within you, and is yours by Divine Right.

AFFIRMATION

(Repeat Twice Daily)

Today, I accept that my every desire is ready to appear in my consciousness, in my life, and in all my affairs. My awareness of Spirit within me lifts me to my highest good.

STATEMENT OF SPIRITUAL TRUTH

(Read Twice Daily)

*"Every thought sets the fulfillment of its desire in motion
in the Mind, so the Mind sees the thing as already done."*

— Ernest Holmes

AFFIRMATIVE PRAYER

(Read Twice Daily)

Today, I accept the presence of Spirit in the world around me and within each person I meet. There is only Spirit, Infinite and Unlimited. It is the source and supply of all things through Its immutable law.

At this moment, I choose to consciously align myself with the Divine Presence that runs through me as joy, harmony, and love. I feel that all the blessings I experienced yesterday are multiplying today. Being one with Spirit, I am open to accept new ideas and new opportunities from sources unknown to me at this time.

Nothing is too great for Spirit to provide, and therefore, I ask for my highest good in all my affairs. I now let Spirit fulfill my desires in surprising and wonderful ways as I act upon intuitive ideas with gratitude and joy.

I am grateful.

And, so it is!

WANT – NOT!

(Read Morning and Evening)

We use the word "want" in our daily conversations without giving much thought to how the Universe perceives it.

As Neale Donald Walsch wrote in his book, *Conversations with God*, *"Saying 'I want more money' only produces the WANTING of more money. It can produce no other thing."*

The word "want" has a strong emotion behind it, and emotion determines our alignment. If you want something, it means you desire what you believe is lacking in your life. Your words continue to manifest the lack or the *want,* but not the thing you desire.

There's a funny story about a man who prayed, "God, I really want to win the lottery. I've been asking you for months, but nothing has happened. I really want to win the lottery." God's reply was, "Well, you have to buy a lottery ticket first!"

A better way to ask Spirit for something is to come from a place of gratitude and expectancy. As Neale Donald Walsch says, *"When you thank God in advance for that which you choose to experience in your reality, you, in effect, acknowledge it is already there."*

Therefore, a better prayer for more money would be, "I am blessed with an overflow of abundance in my life, I am grateful for this blessing, I am confident it will continue, and I am open to receive."

Even if you can't yet see the abundance in your life, that which you desire will manifest if you stay in gratitude. You must *feel* it, truly believe it, trust, and have faith that your desire has already manifested in the One Mind. Keep thanking Spirit, and never plead, because begging only reaffirms the problem.

Remember the ancient saying, *"If you have but the faith of a mustard seed, you shall move mountains. You come to know it is there because I said it is there."*

Spirit always says "yes" to your thoughts, words, and desires, as long as you do your part - keep praising the good in your life and be grateful for your blessings.

AFFIRMATION

(Repeat Twice daily)

My feeling of gratitude is powerful. I am thankful for how Spirit is filling my life with endless blessings!

STATEMENT OF SPIRITUAL TRUTH

(Read Twice Daily)

"Thankfulness is the most powerful statement to God; an affirmation that even before you ask, God answers. Therefore, never supplicate. Appreciate."

— Neale Donald Walsch

AFFIRMATIVE PRAYER

(Read Twice Daily)

I accept there is one Creative Cause, One Mind, One Life, One Loving Presence, that fills all of creation. It creates from perfection, goodness, abundance, and beauty. I am created out of this Loving Presence and accept It as the Source of all my blessings.

I understand this All-Powerful Infinite Energy reflects back to me my emotions, words, and thoughts in powerful demonstrations. I accept that all blessings come from this One Source. As I express my gratitude, Spirit blesses me with more goodness, joy, abundance, and love.

I know this to be so.

And, so it is!

HERE WE GO AGAIN:
THOUGHTS CREATE YOUR LIFE!

(Read Morning and Evening)

Wayne Dyer said that when you change the way you look at things, the things you look at change, and when you change your thinking, you change your life.

The ease with which you can make changes in your life depends on how ready you are to shift. With awareness and practice, change is possible and well worth the effort.

Your life experiences reflect whether you live from a positive or negative viewpoint. It is the Law of Cause and Effect, we cannot manipulate the outcome. For every effect there is a cause; and for every cause, there is an effect.

Your thoughts, behaviors, and actions (vibrations), create specific effects that manifest and create your life as you know it. You are always causing something to manifest in your life by the thoughts you think and the words you speak.

Thought (cause) = Experience (effect)

Our energy, thoughts, words, ideas, and even different types of music, can alter the molecular structure of the elements around us and our physical bodies.

The Creative Life Force within you has no limitations. It is willing to give you all that you desire, always saying "yes" to you, but It can only create for you what It can create *through* you, and It is only limited by your mental acceptance and readiness level.

If you repeatedly complain about your lack of abundance or success, love, relationships, health, etc., then the Law says, *"Okay, I hear you. Stand back and receive MORE of exactly that."* Your vibrational alignment makes it so.

On the other hand, when you move your thoughts to higher ground, the Law responds accordingly. The Creative Force within you, united with the Law of Cause and Effect, is capable of taking the mental form of your desire and turning it into an amazing, life-changing, powerful, demonstration.

AFFIRMATION

(Repeat Twice Daily)

I am observing my highest thoughts in order to support my vibrant health, abundant finances, and freedom of creative expression.

STATEMENT OF SPIRITUAL TRUTH

(Read Twice Daily)

"We are what we think.
All that we are arises with our thoughts.
With our thoughts, we make our world."

— Siddhartha Gautama (the Buddha)

AFFIRMATIVE PRAYER

(Read Twice Daily)

I accept there is one Powerful Infinite Energy that fills all time and space in the Universe. I am the individualized creation and consciousness of this Divine Creator.

I fully realize that my thoughts and words form the conditions and experiences of my life. Spirit hears me and responds according to my expectations. Today, I open myself to the wisdom of the Divine within me. As my word goes into the Law of Mind, I am confident there is no limit to how Spirit will enrich my life in amazing and creative ways.

I release, let go, and let Spirit do the work.

And, so it is!

TO FLOW IN ABUNDANCE

(Read Morning and Evening)

What goes around, comes around; everything in nature moves in circles. The more you give, the more you receive, because you are keeping the abundance of the Universe circulating. In previous chapters, we have talked about how money is energy. If you stop the flow of money (energy) by hoarding, for example, you stagnate or cut off the flow of this gift for others...and yourself.

As Deepak Chopra says in *The Seven Spiritual Laws of Success*, *"In reality, receiving is the same as giving, because giving and receiving are aspects of the flow of energy in the universe. If you stop the flow of either one, you interfere with nature's intelligence."*

I recall an article about a woman who ordered a latte from a drive-thru coffee shop in Florida. When she paid for her drink, she also paid for the coffee order of the driver behind her, who then did the same for the next customer. The employees kept a tally, and by the end of the day, 378 people paid for the order of the stranger behind them. Talk about *paying it forward!*

This is an example of how to keep your blessings flowing. **Pay It Forward Day** is a worldwide celebration of kindness that takes place every year on April 28th.

If you desire more love, give more love; if you desire to be appreciated more, then offer that appreciation to others. Even a silent prayer for someone is a very powerful way to give. As you learn to offer others what you seek, your life will begin to flow in abundance.

AFFIRMATION

(Repeat Twice Daily)

I am sustained by the Divine Energy that flows through my life as joy, kindness, love, and abundance. As I share my good, it returns to me multiplied by ten.

STATEMENT OF SPIRITUAL TRUTH

(Read Twice Daily)

"The more you give, the more you will receive, because you will keep the abundance of the universe circulating in your life."

— Deepak Chopra

AFFIRMATIVE PRAYER

(Read Twice Daily)

Spirit is the divine and radiant center of Life. It is the Light that moves throughout the Universe in the form of Love, Wisdom, and Perfection. I know that Spirit is the source of my abundance, and that money is God in action.

I accept my true prosperity as perfect health, perfect wealth, and perfect happiness.

My life is more joyous because I am learning to share my blessings with others from my heart.

As I speak these words in faith, I know the unstoppable force of the Universe goes forth to heal, prosper, and bless my life, all of my affairs, and the lives of my loved ones.

I give thanks for all that I have, all that I give, and for all the good I am receiving.

I release and let go.

And, so it is!

GIVE LOVE, RECEIVE BLESSINGS

(Read Morning and Evening)

The best way to add blessings to your life is through love. In their book, *Creating Money*, Sanaya Roman and Duane Packer wrote, *"The more love you send out to the world, the more abundance and miracles you will receive in return. Every time you pay a bill or receive money, consider it a gift of love. Make every exchange of money an opportunity to radiate love to those around you."*

Imagine how peaceful life would be if you consciously remembered to send love when you are out and about in the world. It doesn't mean you necessarily love the person at the checkout counter, but you can send them a silent blessing on their journey, thereby also blessing yourself.

Will Boyajian is a busker (street performer) in New York. He plays his guitar on subway platforms for folks who are waiting for the train. You'd think he does it to earn a living from the loose change passerbys throw into his guitar case, but the sign on the ground next to him actually reads: If you are homeless or need help, please take as much from the case as you need. I just like to play."

The idea came to him as a way to help people in need. He now runs a successful nonprofit organization called *Hopeful Cases,* with many other buskers who perform for charity.

Will says, *"We are New Yorkers who love to play music and care about people in our community."* When they open their instrument cases, they unlock a circle of support between people who give what they can and someone in need. It's a perfect and creative example of offering love to the world. It all begins with having love for yourself.

Louise Hay once said, *"When people start to love themselves more each day, their lives get better. They feel better. They get the jobs they want. They have the money they need. Their relationships either improve or the negative ones dissolve so new ones can begin."*

Spirit loves to bless you with money, with perfect health, and with all of your heart's desires. That's why every time you send out love, you open yourself to receiving love. You set the Law of Attraction into motion for the creation of amazing, uplifting, abundant, and exciting miracles.

What an amazing deal!

AFFIRMATION

(Repeat Twice Daily)

I am love in action. Divine Love, *through* me, is blessing my life with heart-pounding miracles.

STATEMENT OF SPIRITUAL TRUTH

(Read Twice Daily)

There is one Super Power in the world that we <u>all</u> have, and it is called Love!

— *Anonymous*

AFFIRMATIVE PRAYER

(Read Twice Daily)

There is one Presence, one creative Cause in the Universe, and It is created out of, and filled with, Love. All that I am is a reflection of the Divine.

I have been created to love myself and to be able to accept love and give love. My heart and mind are open to how I am *already* blessed, and I am receptive to even more blessings from the Universe. As I send out love, the Universe responds with greater abundance, meaningful relationships, and perfect health. I give thanks for all the blessings and miracles I experience each day.

I believe this to be so.

And, so it is!

MISTAKES HAPPEN: IT IS OKAY

(Read Morning and Evening)

The universe is complete and perfect. Nothing in it has been randomly created, including you. The best way to handle a mistake is to look at it as long as it takes for you to see it as an "accident of judgment." Learn from it, and then focus your attention on where you are headed, not where you have been. In *Happy Little Accidents,* Bob Ross wrote, *"We don't make mistakes, just happy little accidents."*

Paul "Bear" Bryant, former head coach of the University of Alabama football team, amassed six national championships and 13 conference championships in his 25-year tenure. When he showed the young players on his team footage of their games, he focused only on the plays where they excelled, and excluded any footage of their mistakes. The secret to his success was understanding that you get more of whatever you pay attention to.

Your conscious mind can be compared to a gardener who is always planting seeds. Focusing on your mistakes only plants more seeds of self-doubt and criticism in your subconscious mind, which then influences your future behavior, and you don't even realize it's happening.

When you agonize over a perceived mistake in your past, your subconscious mind is listening, and it will reflect back to you similar experiences in your future. What can you do? Here are a few suggestions:

- Own up to your mistake so that you are not emotionally hiding from it. This helps you take power back over the situation.

- Review the situation to find out why you got the undesired outcome.

- Identify if there is someone with whom you need to speak, or to whom you need to apologize.

- Learn what you need to do differently the next time you encounter a similar situation.

- Forgive yourself, and move on.

In fact, it is essential that you forgive yourself in order to move on. That's how you release yourself from guilt, anger, shame, or any other feeling you attached to the mistake.

You are human; mistakes are inevitable. But remember, you were created out of Love, which means all your so-called "mistakes" are growth opportunities.

Grow on!

AFFIRMATION

(Repeat Twice Daily)

I accept myself unconditionally. I love myself as I am. I forgive myself. Spirit is always with me, directing, guiding, and guarding me as I continue to grow.

STATEMENT OF SPIRITUAL TRUTH

(Read Twice Daily)

"Give your subconscious only suggestions that heal, bless, elevate, and inspire you in all ways. Your subconscious mind cannot take a joke; It takes you at your word."

— Joseph Murphy

AFFIRMATIVE PRAYER

(Read Twice Daily)

The Spirit of God, which is Life, is present everywhere. It is in the air I breathe and in all that I see. There is no place where Life is not.

No matter where I am or in what direction I move, Spirit moves with me. Everywhere I go, Spirit, My Higher Power, protects, guides, and directs my life. I remain open to the wisdom, the kindness, and the love within me, and I know that Spirit never judges me. I am loved unconditionally at all times.

All the answers and solutions I seek come from within, and everything I need comes to me at the right time, in the right space, and in perfect sequence. I give thanks that all is well in my world.

I affirm that all is well.

And, so it is.

GOOD HEALTH IS ABUNDANCE

(Read Morning and Evening)

Being prosperous and financially wealthy is just one aspect of abundance, a healthy lifestyle is another. And just like negative self-talk can be financially detrimental, your physical well-being and health are also impacted by your self-talk.

In her book, *You Can Heal Your Life,* Louise Hay says, *"We create every so-called 'illness' in our body. The body, like everything else in life, is a mirror of our inner thoughts and beliefs."* Louise believed your body is always talking to you. And if you listen, you can hear it responding to your every thought and word you speak.

When my friend Patricia fell down some stairs and broke her ankle in three different spots, instead of calling it *The Terrible Accident,* she dubbed the experience, *The Great Ankle Adventure of 2014!* Patricia embraced it as an opportunity to experiment with using vibrational power to promote healing. She blessed what she called her Recovery Tools: the splint, the cast, the walker, the boot, the cane, and the rehab exercises. She made up silly songs about healing, and she praised her recovering bones, skin, and nerves. Patricia never complained. She repeated the word "healing" like a mantra. Every aspect of *The Adventure* played a part in her healing.

Her doctor and the rehabilitation therapist, both with decades of medical experience between them, said they had never seen anyone heal as quickly as she had, and with less pain. Patricia told me, *"I aligned myself with the energy of Divine Healing, and focused on the positive feeling of my ankle being fully restored to perfection long before it was healed. Anyone can do this!"*

Emotions such as resentment, anger, fear, or guilt, are vibrational resistance, taking you out of alignment with the Divine Flow. These lower vibrations, when not allowed to evolve, can cause major problems in your body. The same is true with feelings of doubt about yourself if you believe that you are not good enough, smart enough, creative enough... the list goes on.

You were born out of Love, the Creator, and Love never judges, condemns, or criticizes. Evaluate what you say about yourself, and if it's negative, don't worry; thoughts *can* be turned into more positive feelings about yourself.

If a negative thought comes in, take a deep breath, pause, and do your best to not give it any power. It may be challenging at first, but you can do it. Just keep saying, *"I approve of myself,"* over and over again.

There is no way to separate your mind from your body. The abundance of good health that you seek begins when you take mental control over negative self-talk. Staying connected to Spirit through loving thoughts about yourself will jump-start your journey to a new, energetic, healthy, and vibrant life.

And that, my friend, defines abundance!

AFFIRMATION

(Repeat Twice Daily)

I approve of myself. I respect myself. My self-esteem is high because I honor myself.

STATEMENT OF SPIRITUAL TRUTH

(Read Twice Daily)

"The most important thing to remember in our efforts to be good to our body, is to love it. In order to heal ourselves, it is essential to remove the negative beliefs that contribute to unhealthy physical conditions."

— Louise Hay

AFFIRMATIVE PRAYER

(Read Twice Daily)

I recognize there is One Life present everywhere, filling all space and time. I accept that I am created out of this One Life, and am forever unified with this One Life.

As an individualized creation of God, I know perfect health is my Divine Right, and I am receptive to the healing energies in the Universe. The cells of my body are constantly being renewed with new life. I release any self-limiting thoughts that keep my body from healing. I honor and love my body, and I am grateful for my life. I give thanks for my blessings.

I accept my perfection as my truth.

And, so it is!

"HOW?"
IS NEVER THE QUESTION!

(Read Morning and Evening)

When you decide on the life you want, or when you have a specific desire in mind, you typically wonder, *How* is it ever going to happen?

But *How* your manifestation will come forth is not your business. Your job is to declare your desire to the One Mind with feeling and passion, and then shift into a state of allowing. After that, you need to get out of the way so Spirit can do the work.

One of the bestselling books on manifestation is *Ask and It is Given: Learning How to Manifest Your Desires* by Esther and Jerry Hicks. In the book, the creative process to manifest your desires consists of three steps:

1. Your Work: ask for what your desire.

2. Not Your Work: the Universe says Yes, and the answer is given.

3. Your Work: receive and accept the answer given.

The Universe is vast, creative, capable, loving, and very willing to handle all that you ask for, be it the tiny, seemingly insignificant desires, or the big, wild, and crazy wishes.

That's because the Universe does not differentiate between massive oak trees and tiny ants. Think about something good that unfolded in your life where none of the events leading up to it could have possibly been imagined. You couldn't have predicted it, and you don't need to know the *how* in order to believe that anything you want is possible.

As my friend Andee says, "Jesus only had 12 followers and look what he accomplished! Do you actually think he asked *How* his message would reach the rest of the world?"

All manifestations are important. Small manifestations, like finding a parking space, add to your confidence in the power of your connection to Spirit. You begin to realize that you are not alone on this spiritual journey; you have a Partner who knows exactly when and how to deliver your request.

As you broaden your imagination of what your life can *really* be like, it becomes a whole new adventure. Whether you imagine a more creative or affluent career, a new love in your life, a riverboat cruise down the Danube, or a bright, shiny, cherry-red Tesla. Go for it!

You are not alone in your desires. Spirit is right there with you, saying, *"Yes, my beloved, I know how to do this. Now, please, sit back, and prepare to be amazed!"*

AFFIRMATION

(Repeat twice daily)

Today, I accept perfect health, creative opportunities, and amazing abundance with complete trust that the Divine knows exactly *how* to deliver.

STATEMENT OF SPIRITUAL TRUTH

(Read Twice Daily)

"Once you make a decision,
the universe conspires to make it happen"

— Ralph Waldo Emerson

AFFIRMATIVE PRAYER

(Read Twice Daily)

There is one Universal Life, God, Spirit, complete within Itself as Endless Possibilities and Infinite Wholeness. My life is part of this Universal Life. Peace, harmony, and love are manifesting in and through me in absolute perfection.

All things are possible for me because the Power within me does the work. This Divine Intelligence working through me always knows exactly what I need. I receive my Good every day from this unfailing and perfect Creator.

Today, I let go of asking *how*. I turn to the Divine Depth within me that heals, prospers, and blesses me in many amazing ways.

I am grateful for my life.

And, so it is!

ALLOW YOUR ABUNDANCE

(Read Morning and Evening)

Before you can have more money, for example, you must know the real source of it all. To gain abundance, it is vital to first realize and accept that there is a constant, ever-present reality of Divine substance manifesting into form *through your thoughts and beliefs.* If poverty-consciousness keeps you working harder or longer hours, your abundance level will stagnate and never increase. Feelings of unworthiness or the *I-never-have-enough-syndrome,* will perpetuate and simply keep you frustrated and hopeless.

The way to break that vicious circle is to accept that as a child of the Universe, you are automatically *entitled* to your highest good. You have a right to claim perfect health, loving relationships, and financial freedom.

Recognize the Divine as the source of your abundance, and understand that abundance comes to you in many forms; it is not always in the form of money. To be abundant, you must learn to recognize and receive *all* your good.

For many years, I rejected compliments from people instead of simply saying, *"Thank you."* I was blocking my good until I realized that if I cannot accept a simple compliment, then how on earth would I accept all the other blessings that Spirit sends my way?

The Universe does not have attitudes, it has laws. The energy of the Universe is able to support you, but only at the same level you are willing to accept what It is offering without resistance. There must be alignment to create that flow.

You owe it to the Universe to be more open and receptive to the good It is trying to bring you. The Universe always says *Yes* to your every desire. Your job is to say *Yes* to the Universe, which then creates alignment so that abundance can flow your way. That's how you claim your abundance.

And remember, the best response to any compliment is a simple *"Thank you!"*

AFFIRMATION

(Repeat Twice Daily)

I am in harmony with the giving and receiving nature of the Universe. I accept my good in any form, and from wherever it appears.

STATEMENT OF SPIRITUAL TRUTH

(Read Twice Daily)

"If someone says to you, 'I want to give you something' and it is usable, take it. If it is not usable, take it anyway and give it to someone else."

— Raymond Charles Barker.

AFFIRMATIVE PRAYER

(Read Twice Daily)

I acknowledge that there is a loving Presence responsible for all creation. I call It the Divine, Spirit, or the Beloved.

This loving Presence expresses Itself through me, and It is at the very center of my mind and body. I am eternally connected to this Life and can never be separated from It. Today, I am open and receptive for blessings to flow through my life in many forms. Nothing in my thoughts about my future can deny me my highest good.

My future is bright because I know the Universe supports me in all ways, and I accept my blessings with gratitude and appreciation. I give thanks for all that I have, and I say with great expectation, *"More, please."*

I let it be so.

And, so it is!

PROSPERITY IS YOUR DIVINE HERITAGE

(Read Morning and Evening)

In her book, *The Dynamic Laws of Prosperity*, Catherine Ponder says, *"It is your Divine Heritage to be prosperous and have an abundance of good. Your Creator wants you that way. That is the truth about prosperity."*

In order to receive your Divine Heritage, you have to acknowledge the presence, the power, and the intelligence of the Divine as something you can feel and, thus, believe. In this way, you link energies with the Creative Mind and enjoy many blessings as a result.

In 1995, life took an unexpected twist when both Patrick and I lost our jobs. We needed strength and a new way of relating to life. We couldn't imagine why God, the Divine, Universe, Spirit, whatever you want to call It, would breathe life into us, and then just say, *"Sorry, you are on your own!"*

Without the challenge that life gave us, we may have never sought or found the New Thought teachings. We are still learning and growing, finding deeper understanding and acceptance of our Divine Inheritance. Spirit has given us free will to either peacefully or traumatically go through our experiences, even the loss of our jobs.

Positive thoughts fuel powerful principles into existence. Your mind is renewed through positive thinking, expression of faith, confidence, certainty, optimism, and the expectancy of good.

Life is meant to be lived from a place of financial freedom, not "just getting by." We must stay open to all the Universe has to offer us, and experience it fully. Before you see the manifestation of good—money, health, love—you must mentally accept it and emotionally feel it. Catherine Ponder suggests three steps to prosperity:

- Become definite about your desires and write them down.

- Be assured the Universe can then be definite in delivering your desire.

- Create a vision board with your intentions and goals; make it fun and colorful!

Repeat daily affirmations because your words have power. Accept that you are an immensely important individualized creation of Spirit, loved beyond measure, and worthy of your Divine Heritage.

Put these tools into practice to create amazing experiences in your life. The Universe is waiting!

AFFIRMATION

(Repeat Twice Daily)

I am receiving my highest good. I am receiving all that is mine by Divine Right. I am receiving all the abundance the Universe has intended for me – right now.

STATEMENT OF SPIRITUAL TRUTH

(Read Twice Daily)

*"You rob no person when you discover your own good.
You limit no person when you express a greater degree
of livingness. You harm no one by being happy. You steal
from no one by being prosperous. You hinder no person's
evolution when you consciously enter into the kingdom of
your good and possess it today."*

— Ernest Holmes

AFFIRMATIVE PRAYER

(Read Twice Daily)

There is one Presence, one creative Cause in the Universe,
and It is Spirit. It is a moving, flexible, fluid Presence, alive
with life, richness, and abundance.

All that I am is a reflection of Spirit. It created me to act
through me and fill my life with the abundance that is mine
by Divine Right. Therefore, I am receptive to Its abundance
and to Its circulation in my life in all forms, including money.
Money is God in action. I completely accept this idea of
money circulating freely in-and-out of my life, blessing me
with amazing abundance, and allowing me to bless others.

As I release these words of Truth unto the Law, I know that
what lies before me is a rich, full, and abundant life.

I accept this as already so.

And so, it is!

SELF-LOVE

(Read Morning and Evening)

I'd like to close our 30-day spiritual journey together with a personal and important subject to consider: loving yourself.

Problems and challenges, from poor health to difficult relationships, hard situations, or lack of money, could all be corrected by giving yourself approval, acceptance, and love.

To love yourself more, use positive and powerful affirmations that support your development of self-confidence and self-esteem. As Louise Hay recommended in her books, stand in front of a mirror and regularly repeat the affirmations out loud to yourself. The mirror will reflect back to you the very thoughts and feelings you need to believe about yourself to have the joyous and fulfilling life you want.

When something good happens in your life, go to the mirror and say, *"Thank you."* If something not-so-good happens, go to the mirror and say, *"It's okay, I still love you."*

It may be uncomfortable at first, or even difficult to face yourself in the mirror and say, but if you keep at it, your reflection will become your friend instead of enemy.

Amazing demonstrations can come from aligning your thoughts with how Spirit views you; loving yourself in all situations. You are magnificent and worthy of love.

Even if you have been criticizing yourself for years, life can improve as you gently and slowly change your perception of yourself. As Louise Hay says, *"What we think about ourselves becomes our truth. We are dealing with a thought, and a thought can be changed."*

In closing, I am sending you love and light.

May you have miraculous demonstrations on your spiritual journey.

May you be well.

May you love and be loved.

And may your life be filled with abundant joy, peace of mind, perfect health, and happiness.

You deserve it!

AFFIRMATION

(Repeat Twice Daily)

In the infinity of life where I am, all is perfect, whole, and complete. My self-esteem is high because I honor who I am.

STATEMENT OF SPIRITUAL TRUTH

(Read Twice Daily)

"Through the power of love, we can let go of the past and begin again. Love heals, forgives, and makes whole."

— Ernest Holmes

AFFIRMATIVE PRAYER

(Read twice daily)

I recognize that this Universe has been created out of a Presence that knows only Love. The love of Spirit is the underlying principle of all life.

This Presence is personal to me, because it loves and moves within me as Divine Right Action. I can never be separated from God's loving presence. Today, I listen with complete faith and trust to the voice of Love as It always guides me in all ways.

I accept the abundant good that is flowing easily and freely within me. As I love myself, I offer love to others, knowing we are all one in Spirit. With gratitude and joy, I accept the eternal love of the Divine.

I absolutely know this to be so.

And, so it is!

ABOUT THE AUTHOR

Jan Lynch has been a student of New Thought for 25 years. She is a licensed Spiritual Practitioner at the Awakening Ways Spiritual Community in Atascadero, California. She is also the co-author of *Affirm Your Future: How to Use Affirmations to Bridge Your Future.*

Lynch has served on the Board of Directors of local humane societies for several years, organizing fundraisers and fostering hundreds of kittens until they are old enough to be adopted. She lives on the Central Coast of California with her husband Patrick and a house full of pets.

ACKNOWLEDGMENTS

Rev. Dr. Terry zumMallen and Rev. Dr. Frank zumMallen, I am forever grateful for your support.

Sincere appreciation to my longtime friend, Andee Allan, whose sense of humor kept reminding me to calm down and "just write the book" whenever I began to doubt myself.

This book was enriched by my editor, Patricia Alexander, and her deep spiritual understanding of the New Thought teaching. Thank you, Patricia for your ideas and patience.

I am grateful for my wonderful husband who constantly encouraged me to create this body of work.

Without Hawkeye Publishers, this book would still be in the thinking stage.

And thank you, the reader, for taking this journey with me.